SLOW DANCE ON STILTS

SLOW DANCE ON STILTS

poems

marie jordan

For information and permission to
reproduce selections from this book, write to
Permissions/ Poets Press,
P. O. Box 897, La Jolla, CA 92038

Publisher's Cataloging-in-Publication
(Provided by Quality Books, Inc.)

Jordan, Marie.
Slow dance on stilts : poems / by Marie Jordan.—
1st ed.
p. cm.
LCCN 2001-086942
ISBN 0-931721-17-2

1. Twenty-first century--Poetry. I. Title.
PS3560.0753S56 2001   811'.6
QB101-700180

Distributed by
Baker & Taylor Books
50 Kirby Avenue
Somerville, N.J. 08876
Tel: 800 775-1100

book design
and cover art (with the help of
gravestone rubbings and a flash light)
by Mick Haggerty

La Jolla
POETS PRESS
Kathleen Iddings, Editor

acknowledgements

Some poems in this collection have appeared in:
New Letters, Aurora, The Eleventh Muse, Windhover, the Onset Review, Rattle, The Spoon River Poetry Review, California State Poetry Quarterly, Mindscapes, Tidepools, New Texas , The Poetry Conspiracy, and *Concho River Review*.

With many thanks for grants from the *AAUW* and *the Vermont Studio Center*.

for Christa and Liza

contents

SLOW DANCE ON STILTS

THE CUTTING DOWN OF ALL MY TREES

You didn't have to go and do that,
cut them down.
I'm losing parts of me daily,
like the sparkle of the eye,
my hunger for hyperbole, and a slow
dance on stilts, oh I've changed
since you cut down my trees. I'm counting

      the losses on this hill where
      white stumps of my slain trees
remain, reckless grave markers, where dazed
      birds peck at the aged ice plant & weeds
      grow thick like cotton sweaters. But
      young men

still arrive with presents and shaved chins.
When they walk there's music in the backs of their legs,
they go to the theatre and vacation in France. They grow hair
on their chests like scarlet bouquets of phlox and primrose,
their shoulders move with confetti peach smoothness,
there are tiger lilies and thunder in their stomachs.
They come here looking for trees.

The hill has grown muddy, uncertain,
I lose both feet in the climb. I can't climb.
My tongue dries and curls like a leaf under the mower.
The bodies of the dead trees are stacked
like casualties of war and I want to lay myself
on them, I want my photograph taken that way
to remind myself later

      that I once knew pleasure, I once rushed at the sky like trees do,
with a confutation of green. Once I sprawled
      into solid earth with thistledown fingers, I clapped
      my feet in the air, I gathered loves and tumbled
      moist in lady slippers and clover
up to my knees. I had so many arms, like Arabian nights,
and when the sun turned its face to this hill
      my arms shone like the pink hibiscus
      sleeves of bridesmaids for men to fling
      and tie their ropes on the gallows of the temporary
      before hanging themselves.

ALMOST

This isn't the way it was supposed to be,
anybody will tell you that. Me, the peasant queen,
        you banging away at your life,
breaking the backs of bulls, dancing
        on the ribs of dead horses—
        are we sick of love yet? I want
to go back to November, to Oaxaca,
        to the women who braided my
hair and massaged your temples
        while we played guitars
and sang Las Mañanitas to each other just because
        we knew the words. I refuse to
be a part of your biography, you who
        wore neglect as a talisman and stopped
listening for the songs the children sang.
        Now you move toward the water
        and your gravy spine is giving
you pain. I once got chills when I touched you
        where your neck curls down like a worm
to the curve and sprawl of your chest. I climbed
        you like a tree. Where did we
        lose it? Swamp talk, beach and mud snails
will always make me think of you, such cowards
        in the storm—I won't forget
we found the perfect shell
        and in its ear almost lived forever.

THAT KIND OF WOMAN

Where I am
I am what is missing.
—Mark Strand, "Keeping Things Whole"

She was that kind of woman who
could nurse a baby while driving a pickup
down the 405 to Chula Vista. She had a way
of tuning into sounds, like wind.
She knew which tone of voice to use
when calming brush storms, the desert flood of dust
that threw itself on us every August.
She joked about her working relationship
with trees, was aware of their favorite poems.

Then the old man flew the coop, just up and left,
and she lost the old ease of moving
inside the wind, of identifying river blossoms.
It was the sound of her kids crying in the other room
that tore her up. Crying in the same room
where he left his new phone number
with *her* name on it.

She blamed herself, began to mistrust forests
stopped camping by the river with the children,
and sold the truck. She wanted to know things
like how to walk around the world one small step
at a time and how to merchandise inner beauty
and slow dance with God. But she was broken-
axled, out of music, mud stuck to her brow
and she forgot how to change a tire.

When you have good kids you have it all,
she realized, and hitched her wagon to an idea.
Off they drove in a Chevy station wagon,
an Abrahamette leading her flock across the desert
of make-believe, the kids playing I See Something Blue
and singing songs their Mama taught them
when she was somebody's wife.

They boogied with the mules at Grand Canyon
and flew to the moon from the Space Age

Motel in Gila Bend, the first of many flights
to places requiring wings of fiction.

Now she longs to lie awake by a stream
with them again, swim in black mountain lakes,
listen to their song— saved from the surrender.
But the trips to Venus with Mom are kid stuff now.
Kisses like soap bubbles, and journals crowded
with names of battles won are packed away
with the boxes of drawings and painted stone.
Cartwheels lie behind on the grass at the river's edge.

She's that kind of woman who can partner with silence
while driving the 405 to Los Angeles until the voices
come, the ones that calm the storms and sing without chains:
Where we are there is nothing missing.

A STRETCH

We eat dinners,
toast, sing,
dance. We swim too, dive,
dig, crave for more. A scrappy moon
tonight and so many songs tugging
the roiling spiny mass in the long stomach
        of God,
the last frontier.

SURVIVAL MONOLOGUE

1

Things are what they are. Doorknobs, chairs, window
ledges, beds, chins and noses, the painted eyes of Sicilian
carts. A wall heavy with fish nets. I could fade,
fade like newsprint, like scattered orange peels. The ladies
are wearing pink today. Pink, the color of the underside
of wrists, pink like velvet roses on flat wire stems.

I'm unraveling shrines formed of kasha and polenta.
I once celebrated the names of ships in the port of Palermo.
I sew flags at night. Broad banners of branch thorns,
my fingers are snails, I smell of cigars. The ladies are drinking
espresso in china cups delicate enough for the lips of spiders.

2

Don't look at me. The ladies look at me. They watch me
diminish. They think I am not layered in cinnamon, nor
lacquered in iced coral. They believe it is too late for me
to scale stones, dress myself in the whistle of a train or wear
cashmere. Don't they know I want a hat like theirs? I imagine
changing my name, learning a new alphabet, the plié
and three-minute mile. I live in a slush of sunsets and I dream
of lily-eyed princes. My body is still in process of becoming.

3

The ladies are white. White like galloping Desdemonas,
white like chrysanthemums and typing paper. The Sicilians,
sons and daughters of Saracens, Arabs and Spanish
conquerors, are brown. Brown like cappucino. My mother
is brown. Brown like halvah. I am brown.
Brown as the tongues of the dead.

I paint myself in tertiary colors in order to enter the earth,
hear its secrets, wear the scent of the *Conca d'Oro* , learn
the sigh of the widow iris and Sicilian melons
ripening in the sun. I could bleach easily. I am not
unusual. I am one of many countries and many faces.
The ladies pump the sun, they stain their underwear.

I became an adult by continual dissociation. There are
fictions in which I am the beloved. I begin
to draw maps of cities and towns and villages,
places I've never been. I draw
pretty houses and shops and cafés on the page,
it's the way of fiction.

The people in these towns play musical instruments and sing
canzoni of found and lost love. They speak the language
of boats.The voice is the blood of the bougainvillea and
basilico, I lie down in the ambrosia of Termini Imerse
at dusk. I sip zibibbo and watch the ladies. Tomorrow
I will move up to piecework. My flags will fill the cellars
of captains. I'm growing up, up, the way Santa Rosalia
asks of me, the wooden pupi in the piazza will forget my voice.
I will go to America.

4

America! The ladies turn to look at me. Their clothes are lighted
windows. Their faces are enormous grapes. It is not spectacular
for them to ride a bus or request change. I wear the leather boots
of one who sews flags, but I work in a restaurant — the *cozze* is cotton,
the lemons are coarse as an old man's foot. Ladies stroll the beach

in their new shoes and hats of white. I suddenly
understand the terrible sadness of wealth without
knowledge. I am one of the many small blazes that singe

borders. I'm alone and yet held fast in the corrugated
palms of dead mammas and nonnas whose prayers
ignited the churches photographed by tourists.
It is the noon of my life and the world is not so unhappy
or happy, not so good or bad, not so beautiful or ugly. I unpack
my baskets, I serve the *cacciatore*. The ladies ask for salt.
    I give them what they want.

IMAGINARY LIGHT

Now stop it, I have come to know as of late
fantasies are eternal, they have a life of worth, like
stones and toads and thoughts of humans.
I have seen into the wet bones gathered in place
at your neck which pull together in a tent
when I kiss the moist fixed corners, the edges
that curl, the good lines remaining unchanged.
Some of us are grateful for the sprawling reminders
of morning, for the shape of faith as it unfolds in our hands
the way day lilies open at a single finger of light.

LOVED ONES

My cousin cuts off the heads
in family portraits,
pastes them on different bodies,
and mails them to us

as Christmas cards. This year
I turned up with Aunt Anna's body
drooped from my shoulders
like a muddy swan, her fingers

scratching my chin. What
could I be thinking
with such long bones
as fingers? I can feel

the cool of her pressed sleeves,
the pearled brooch at the neck. But
this neck is is a recitative of a Mozart
opera, spreading and bending

its watery aria, curling around
some major theme, a narrow neck
catching ideas in flight like insects,
a neck that swoops with its own weight,

grasps my jaw for dear life.
Aunt Anna's body crescendoes my face,
my teeth float like lilies, I am possessed.
I wonder how I can remember my name

in this strange orchestration. I want
to shake the trembling fingers
from my cheek, pinch the neat
fluffed breasts, and dance my head

to another frame, perhaps to the smooth
apple body of cousin Noni
on the floor beside
the pant leg of Uncle Bud,

or atop the podium of Aunt Katharine's
regal slump.
Who will we each be next year?
Will Aunt Anna's crushed
velvet bodice torment the beard
of cousin Doug? Whose shoulders

will caress my mother's ears?
— which languid hand with rings

will scratch my pathetic chin?
What things are these, darling and peculiar
we wear as coronets and props? Aliens,
strangers, more dear than we can bare.

ISLAND ARTIST

Akalem paints her house
with grass brushes
and blood-red pigment,
her palms, flat like wood,
work the mud and cow dung,
fingers, tough as rivers
leave a black and white snake
coiled on the wall
with the yellow stripes running
thick and fast as though being chased,
the earth meeting itself

and she becomes an ideogram
in the shadows of the Koran
forbidden to represent
living things. She remembers the men
out fishing and the sea moving in like a boy
lifting his shirt,

and she jerks her shawl
above her nose,
dips her fingers in the paste,
beats it on the wall,
where it loops like eyes
too tired to hang on a face;

later she will gather sticks,
nurse her babies,
kill and cook a chicken,
blow sweat from her lip,
raise a foot to scratch
a splattered toe,
buried in the dust
like a root.

WHERE WARRIORS RUN

Life has no shape. We impose
shape on it so we can deal with it.
—*Arturo Islas*

This is a shape of dying then,
a rock cliff graveled whore
spreading its arms across
an ice-sunk winter plain. A dip
of the tongue into the stream
of its own scars. So this is it.

The man runs down the flat nose of the hill,
toward the barrel of the gun and the point
of a sword, his arms extended, a flurry of questions
chase him like neurotic dogs

and it's raining. It's happening again.
The wind catches his coat, his frown
is full of bad teeth. He's headed
toward the arrow tip, the hill won't budge,
not after what he didn't slay. He thinks

he's dreaming when
over there the Chanke-opi-Wakpala
is thigh deep in human pieces,
a woman parts her hair and shows him the nape

of her neck. A dead man's torch eye catches
him unaware, the mouth open
as in eternal mid sentence; his uniform
is a snake, wants to strangle him. You must despise
or love the ones you kill. If he knew his enemy

he might fall to love. Weapons are gathered
and sold as souvenirs in gifts shops
in the cities. His voice is a closed door shouting no
to a life he can't open or part with. He caresses
the woman, gives himself to experimentation,
enters the swarm of whispers, the present
is his past, repeats itself to the mother
by the linden tree, frozen white, her sucking baby
dead at her breast. The baby wears a tiny beaded cap
sewn with the tattered design of a flag,

Whose party is this? The dying call to him
so he must run, his foot hits the stiff head
of the woman parting her hair and he left his
brain where he is going. It is for this
he runs, the misnamed shapes, the living.

BEACH ENCOUNTER

A man
approaches me on the beach
   to say he can't lie any longer
and he drops to his knees, pounds his fists
   on the sand. He takes hold
of my legs. His breath spreads
   in a pool at my feet.
I plead with him to rise up, let go,
   try to be sensible, but the man goes on,
   he's wasting his gifts,
he's fed up, he's HAD IT
   and he hits his head against
   the sharp stones of the sea wall.

It's then I feel
   the imposing weight of my own body,
I'm not wearing my dancing shoes.
   I've forgotten my lines. Where has the orchestra
gone? My voice takes on the man's desperation.
   I'm weeping with him.
He's praying for help. I'm praying for help.
   My forehead peels off in slivers.
   I've bloodied my hand in his,
the man's scarf drops from my neck,
   the opening in my head empties out its sand,
   I'm floating
in kelp, in the disembodied acres of wind. I'm
   on my knees.
   The sun turns its face.

MOON BITTEN

I sit by the fan palm out back,
the one I dug up and hauled with me
on each move, its fronds fire green
and decide to drive up the mountain,
listen to country western on the radio,

talk to him, describe the night: Look, Baby,
I'll tell the seat, look how the trees are
moon-bitten, and just listen
to the rhythm of that wind, would
you. It's an asthmatic wind, I'll tell him,
and he'll try to say something funny,

he'll tease me, call me an adjective drunkard,
the worst kind. As a ranger he led classes
in pine identification, doctored coyotes and snakes,
could stick-light a fire and halt a careless swimmer's date
with death, but couldn't stop
disease cells from partying in his chest.

He was talking to God when I last saw
light in his eyes, a man
who glowed blue at the names of insects and trees,
who called animals his kids, and who wanted
to get old with the owls and the juniper.

I'll find the trail where we listened to the hum
and creak of the Torrey Pine, I'll know
the sea spray, the low sand canyon
and its carved hearts, the path
now covered over, like a sleeping child,
with dried scabs of leaves, with weeds.

WOMAN IN LINE AT THE DMV

It's
my life, she said,
the fur & toothless
mouth of the mangy lap dog, it's
my daughter's conversation as she looks
at her watch and asks the time. It's
nine hours of TV and not
laughing once. It's a used book store
and a cashier with psoriasis and hair
like carpet lint who won't look at you; oh

it's last year's knotty poinsettia, people
earning miles of money paying
their bills on time, obtaining drivers
licenses in sunny climates with
loved ones. It's a daughter's pearl eyes

and it's the furnace clearing its throat
into my room at night. It's TV sitcoms
all with the same characters. It's the old dog
hobbling to his dish and lying
            on the floor vent. It's a flea in
the waist band of your jeans. It's
the cat at the window with a starling
in its teeth. It's the stunned eyes
of the starling. It's crusty snow gnarled
around unnameable trees. It's a daughter
with somewhere else to go.

THE GOODBYE

Toulon, France

I'll go on looking out from the lamp
of this camera pretending
        I'm not here &

        grabbing fists of air
& pressing them to my lips with extreme
        tenderness. I am prisoner

                to this expanse of athletic blue,
which is how the port desires to be remembered,

        the port wants to be rocked to sleep,
wants its docks
of steel to hold onto the song and dance a little longer,
        gather the tiny mouths that loved & left.

The moon has an appetite,
        wants to be fed fast,
        its face lipstick-red like noses of circus clowns
slow dancing on stilts, the moon
        is desperate at times.
                If that is

too strange to hear,
        think of a red blood stain on a sliced cube
of chocolate. Think of perspiring decks and smokestacks,
        the chilled neck of a girl at dawn
mounting the gangplank of a Navy destroyer
        to say goodbye to her daddy
her brother
        lover
husband, think
        of the particular color that vanishes the second you
look at it, think of an American-neon-sailor
        reporting for duty today, think of the jellied eyes of tuna
which the proud mothers of Marseilles
        throw to gulls.

        Think of the Enterprise fueling in the port at Toulon.
A bride with a camera, small against the skyline of such a vessel,
        bristles at the underside
of the horizon, you could miss this scene.

Go on snapping photos,
there's not much time. Safe in your palm
           is his blown kiss. He's caught in the guts
of a wave, a war waiting for his body.
           This is not a marriage with skills of flotation.

           One more
kiss.
           In a few miles
he'll be a spec, a thought,
or is that the baby you should have had together?
           Where is he taking the baby? If you think
this is a joke, go ahead,
           blow another kiss
for the empty womb. With every gun blast
           and parting ship they tell you
to be brave.

I MADE LOVE WITH A MONKEY TODAY

I drove
into the indoor parking ramp
painted in Frank Stella blue and pink
with my mother talking the obvious
in the California noon
(Oh, I was desperate for a gazelle
this morning, for the long moans of a dove,
for the kiss of a gorilla, the kind who could
write War and Peace if at the word processor
long enough)

and we're in the Jasper Johns parking ramp
below the Edward Hopper cafe.
I park the car,
and a woman is using her car phone
in the Lexus next to us.
I'm not coming back, she's yelling,
and the baby is hailing drool
on her neck,
you'll never change, that's why, Fred,
this is the last time!
She wants out, and my mother says
things are different
since her day when folks stayed married.
Fred is probably a wolf, she says,
prowling the black hole of desire
starving for a bite of forbidden cake
squeezing his chances where he can,
a guy who treats women like pets.

We emerge from the Sol LeWitt elevator
into the toe of the sun
and my mother wants to eat outside
so we order from a menu
with Leonardo's hand of God
reaching out to Adam on the cover
and that's when I see the monkey --
crouched at the next table.

I refuse to stare
so I turn my head and picture him

hanging from the limb
of the traffic light on the corner,
tiny sharp teeth flashing,
grinning at me

until he breaks into a graceful sway
above the heads and cars
of Camino Del Mar
and everything below pops like blisters
beneath such grace.

I barely speak during the entree
and the restaurant becomes
a Duane Hanson creation,
the waiters, plates, spoons,
tables, all in polyamide
while the monkey
stuffs his mouth with pasta.
My mother says it's disgusting
how some people eat,
he's beautiful says I.

My mother's eyes turn the brown of
certain works of Andy Goldsworthy,
she warns me against what she calls
bad sorts: there are responsible,
men out there. She emphasizes out there
as if referring to someplace authentic like
the Getty's garden
or a peninsula by Cristo.

I burrow into the soft wall
of another thought
where the monkey takes my hand
and I follow,
stumbling behind him
but in step,
I know the dance.
I'm floating,
no, soaring,
like a Jenny Holtzer adage
on a marquee,

I'm soaring in the arms of a monkey
across the tiled plaza,
he & I
and we're burning
in a boiling wasteland of stars!

He kisses me
until I'm strewn across the table
lifeless. I'm cinders,
crushed and powdered,
but he pulls me back with a puff
of his pasta breath,
pulls me into himself
and I'm born inside his body
dangling from his glorious
skinny tail he tells me
words so delirious I drown,
I'm sinking, faster and faster,
I'll love him forever and
love him forever,
this man who eats pasta
like snow.

Back in the car my mother says
I look pale, like a frantic rose and
did I really need two cappucinos?
I'm trembling like a Frances Bacon priest
or a Kim Dingle baby. How can I tell her
nothing matters and everything
does. I'm wild without
him. How can I tell her
I give up, I'm going to join the convent
of the holy order of minimalists.

I give up my perch as
an Annette Messager sparrow
in a sweater. My lovely monkey
has dabbed his mouth with his sleeve
and driven away in his Porsche.
Yes, Mother, yes, yes, I know.
Men are animals.

ABNORMAL CELLS OF
UNDETERMINED SIGNIFICANCE

Someone said lawns are
expressions of soul and spirit,
and back yard gardens
are sacred grounds like musical
events or outdoor concerts, beaded
voices raised in praise ...
      Now
mushrooms invade this temple
lawn, white mouths hissing
through the green waves of grass,
bloated dumpling faces
multiplying fast. I didn't know
about the changing shapes and
sizes of some anomalies. Didn't know
which soil the mushrooms preferred.

      Dirt has no conscience.
      Dirt can betray
and we didn't plan ahead,
didn't prepare. The morning glories
coughed through the first assault, the fichus
suffered nausea, the ferns came down
with laryngitis. We should have
bought terminal grass insurance,
      taken the lawn to church,
done more singing acapriccio,
exercised the lilies more. People tell me
poison mushrooms, these
sporophore heads like knives intent
on eliminating the glassy green,
are God's creation, too.
      So please,
pray with us. Tell God we're aching
for the clean sutures of Spring,
the first choir of tulips in the recovery
room. And then we'll all sing
for Her.

COYOACÁN

Evening unrolls like a rug
in the interior halls of the song god,
his mouth scrolls out the message,
the song will end.

A radio plays Frank Sinatra
in the kitchen where the *cocineras*
roll and fry tortillas. Sunday families
order chilies and *mole* and bottles
of gin. The blond woman had danced
her wedding in this place, and today these families
don't look up from their plates as she passes.
Don't know she has wings on her wrists. She
speaks the language of brooms. The blond woman

listens for Flower and Song, she is wearing
the pitched dust of stone upon stone
from Teotihauacan where she and her *esposo*
had stood atop the jagged temple of the sun
and vowed till death. She can almost hear the flute
playing the flute
on that day, touch the young men
in feathers who kissed her like so many mothers.

She can hear their feet of glass against the floor,
can hear the scratch of starched lace
at her jaw and elbows. But now strangers
sit at the tables, they drink tequila, almond cured
pulque, mugs of beer, they sing *Las Golondrinas* as

people arrive. People leave.
Arrive and leave. I can't hang on to the world
as it spins away, can't part the stones,
stone takes wood, wood takes feather. Feather
takes air, takes night, the voices are smoke,
the men have disassembled their straight line
of gold teeth and neck scarves.

At the table in the center of the room
a family of many sons have picked corn
and yucca to drop along the hallways of Xochipilli.

The blond woman should have known,
should have guessed this time would come,
should have seen the distant trains, the waiting
cactus, the wails of women
sewing white *rebozos* for their sisters.

The *cocineras* chop and stir to the sound of Frank Sinatra
singing "My Way" and know better than she.
If she had only listened, for now the Tlamatinime,
those clever pixies of deities, who believe only art
can save the world, have gone north,
and the blond woman sees this room
as through the grit of a virulent storm.

She returns to the street wearing
the *esposo's* ankle bracelets, she keeps her balance
in the tilt and pulp of the anniversary afternoon
where she once was so certain this place was home.

Mexico City

SAFE IN THE GULL

Her brother promises he won't cry and holds out
for the first few blows, but by the time it's over
his voice is worn like weathered wood. He's eight years old
and dying of old age.

The girl is seven and waits her turn in the room
with the tools. She watches the screwdrivers, pliers,
hammers and drills on their safe hooks and their cozy homes
on shelves. The girl thinks maybe the hammer would like to drive

a nail into something, wonders if it wants to split
something apart— but the hammer is quiet.
She whispers to the tools, to the sledge hammer, ball-peen,
tack hammer and claw, but they pretend they can't hear.

The router, the plane, the rasp and hedge shear feign sleep.
She calls to the nippers, the tweezers, the clamps and the tongs,
the vises and tape rolls, cutters and bolts. She pleads with the pliers,
 the rivets, the nails, washers and locks. Please, she cries.

On the high wooden table a level, with its yellow bubbles like
floating eyes, lies on its side as if dead. Who will help me escape?
she asks as if dreaming. Not the dead level, not the sleeping stapler,
not the calipers, the clamps. Not the nails.

Does the scissors want to cut something? The girl will run
through the garage wall, crawl into a hole outside, keep crawling
to where her mother will be waiting with the story books. Her mother will
tell her the one about

the sea gulls who store food in their bellies to eat later. The girl
will crawl through the hole and come out on the other side, find her
mother. She'll be like Alice, like the four kids of Narnia.
She will come out of the hole to her mother and the beach

where the hungry eye of the gull will be glad to see her,
and she will become small enough to fit inside the belly
of the gull. Her brother is wiping his face with his t-shirt. She is no
longer afraid. She will become small enough to fit inside

the dining hall belly of a gull so when the door opens,
she'll be safe in storage. But what is this terrible protest
from the tools? They scream in voices like children!
Tears storm the concrete floor.

The hammer squashes the nut of the gull's eye,
breaks bashes its pink neck, bashes the shaking layer of feathers,
the papery legs.

YOU'VE GOT MAIL

             I'd like
to ask where
             these small clots
are taking us, like spoiled corners
             of an old Spanish verb book,
                     amo, amo,
(te) amo. I ask the ink of moon why
                     this mess of flesh sinks
             into itself in waves of so lonesome
             a sea, each night stalks of scrub weed
go on scrubbing while
                     the moon stinks of silence
and each morning to
             read again
             simple as pulping a *bendición*
& stepping on the soft spongy spine of a thesaurus,
— A clamor of missives,
                     Save-As-New, clickitty-clack.
             What's a reflection
             of our real selves, our us?
Te amo, mi amor.

PICASSO'S WEEPING WOMEN

"Picasso and the Weeping Women"
exhibition, the Los Angeles County Museum of Art

Here we have Dora,
teeth bumping into her mantilla,
the painted fingers gouging
the soft pyramid of her throat,
And over there Olga, so many
pieces of her, with Marie Therésa,
eyes stuck through with nails
both wearing day dresses
sewn with pin spikes—
which war is this?
See the wall
with a photograph of Guernica
projected? — its images
blurred, making the whole thing
appear under water
with human chests laid
like little boats at the bottom
of the sea while the women
scream,

pull out their hair,
claw their cheek flesh,
their dissected parts
dropping like gulls, wing-snapped,
eyeballs lying in corners
in shards,
the splintered lover's jaw,
gaping chest and legs spread
like plans sprung. If this
is love it can start an illness. Breasts
& thighs with little tumors
needing surgery. Love is illness
itself, each Weeping Woman's
tear with its own charity hospital.
Weeping women,
we'll always have them.

HERRING

1

11:00 o'clock and the morning is sewn together
in uneven stitches, edges embroidered
by a blind person. By noon everything could
lose the pattern, its strings could unravel,
but I think today is different. At five years old
a girl doesn't consider implications.

I pull up on tiptoe, I yank a braid, pull
at ribbons. Outside it's white, white as a clenched
knuckle, white as bleached cotton panties,
new anklets from Woolworth's.

2

The neighborhood transforms itself to
radiant fields of iced parking lots,
and galvanized sidewalks. A stirring
of sewer rats warm their bellies on pipes
in the basement. Rabbits and squirrels lie
impaled in snow outside by the fence,
their dead eyes spiked open as in greeting.

3

ll:05 and my father will notice me.
I am good. I am funny. I make him laugh
by standing on a chair before him in the kitchen
and stuffing an entire jar of pickled herring
down my mouth.

His laughter dashes the walls, moves
through the pale rooms, stuns the parrot
next door who sniffs the air and asks what's that
smell. Laughter that never gets the spots
out of clean hands, that scares the folk upstairs.

Minneapolis becomes a city of laughter,
all fathers laughing at once, laughing their throaty,
ribald way, falling down laughing, me
eating pickled herring, packing pickled herring
in my cheeks, chewing, swallowing, asking
for more. Laughter rushing over the dishes
in the sink, yellow cupboards, the table with its

flowered oilcloth, laughter
like jars tumbling from tall shelves.

4

My hands are paper geraniums,
they pop up in the snow— my thoughts are swag-bellied,
like ice giants who play tricks on foolish children
who eat herring for their daddy's attention,
they hunt down little girls with braids and pretty ribbons,
the one who eats a jar a day.

5

The aunties eat in Chinese restaurants
and smoke cigarettes. Shadows
of a mother move along the walls
like smoke. She rises out of reach
onto the back of the dragon painted
on the shade of the hanging lamp.
She is far away, at the center of the place
where light originates.

The aunties eat vegetarian
egg rolls. They know
nothing of pickled herring.
The mother ignores the little girl,
sips weak tea.

6

Let me swing my braid for you,
untie my ribbons. Let me show you
my tight rope act, I'm a ballerina, a magician,
I'm the girl who memorizes verse. See?
I'm smart. I'm funny.

7

The mother folds her eyes. Her breathing
shifts. Forgod'ssakeshutup. She is speaking
to her egg roll, I believe. Or the fish-eyed dragon
of the hanging lamp. She won't save me. She has
ribbons of her own.

A BORROWED LIFE

The marbled eye of God, busy with the sparrow,
the lily & the camel
caught in the squeeze of a needle, turns
again, our lives are not our own. I could have
given it back, gotten the right
one, but I paused a little too long
to listen to the battering of a street drum
and a poem recited by a tree. I stopped to eat
a bowl of seasons in the form of eighth notes
which I now wear around my waist despite
the noise. Shoulders crack like twigs—
a spine shifts in letters of the alphabet,
colors are assigned to empty spaces. Eyes
droop like a soft purse, the coins of another life
spill out.

THUNDERING TIGERS

What can endure when crickets
do all the talking? The foreigners arrive
where geese sleep on contaminated rivers
with the frogs, where a crane
gathers bones with its sleeve and
ants and mosquitos grow big as thumbs.

The air is webbed, woven in steam,
tight hot threads of air flume around the heads
of the travellers, swamp enters their boots,
peels the polish off the lady's toes.

A sagging hevea tree rubs its eye
in the sun like a man with cataracts.
You'll find frogs east of Java
and the geese tell stories
of naked rice farmers while women
wearing *ikat* red silks bear jars on their heads,
babies slung to their spines, their whispers
like *cinchona* clung to a fever.

A native mother cries for bread,
her tears are fierce, her tears are tigers.
Tigers storm the sand as a crane sniffs the backs
of the foreigners' knees and the lady loses her breath
to a young man with a palm leaf on his head.
She's exposing her teeth. Her hands turn to ponds
in the shadow of the volcano, she'd like her photo taken

with him. Nearby water buffalo
pantomime a *wayang purwa* shadow play
and the bamboo roofed temple sings
in sacred trees. Clouds stick to the sky like wet maize;
a wrinkled shirt of a sky surrounds the volcanic mess
of mountains across the Lombok straits without a care

for the keepers of goats who have not discovered
digital. Tomorrow the river will flood
and children will maneuver the buffalo carts and
machetes while their stories take flight like wild parrots.

The visitors have no patience for rain, swampmeat & song,
can't hear the dance of the temple, the geese, the frogs
and crane. The tigers will go on thundering
when the visitors leave with their photos and rashes,
their groans of relief and wallets safe in their ears. Tigers remain.

BREAKING THE SILENCE

Sometimes I think the helmet of morning
        is too big for me, covering
        all of the all of the nothing which is
me
        and here at this moment I forget
        the order of obscurity,
        my poor excuses.
                It's an ignoble
                        glory, this quickened heartbeat,
the desire for you that tastes
        like apples. Your fingers are those
        of the shadow puppets
                here now under pin spots in La Costa.
Hurry, let's light the last lamp, be glad again
        for words unsaid
        at last spoken because
you love me.

CHICLETS IN GUADALAJARA

I sit on a park bench
reading Neruda and a boy
not as tall as my hip
comes to me, stands very close,

says, Cheeklets?

He presses his face to mine,
eyes so near I see four of them,
Cheeklets? again.

Across the promenade
another boy skips around white-skirted
trees while his young parents coo
and titter at him from their blanket
on the grass.

A man staggers by the fountain,
drunk this early morning, hikes
his trousers,
vomits in the pool
and a cloud of butterflies
dash for the sky.

The boy
rolls his hand against my arm,
he smells of burnt hair. He drops
the gum in my hand, Cheeklets?

His old person baby breath hot against
my chin. Such a face
must have been invented in committee
where movie image makers
perfect the look of a child
whose job is to yank from an audience
its dopey but passionate
sighs. I should lift
him to my lap:

*It's time for our story
and our napsie, little fella...*

The man at the fountain snarls
at air, punches at something invisible,

staggers, falls. *¡Vente!*

The boy's hand tightens on my arm,
Cuanto? I say, as if asking a secret.

The man at the fountain
negotiates a cigarette to his mouth,
sets fire to a match. *Cinco peso.*
The boy holds up five fingers.

He runs, head down, bare feet thudding,
to the man and they vanish
in the shadows of the skirted trees.
The pavement and the fountain close
around the space where they were.

The young parents across the promenade
play peek-a-boo with their child
from their nest of sweaters
and shoes, bottled milk, sugar
buns. The sweaty package of gum
sits on my lap.

Sunlight collapses
into the grass; crippled, irresponsible
birds peck at weeds
in an afternoon impotent & unarmed.

THINK NO FURTHER

1
This rain is
a staircase
creaking, crumbling,
          breaking apart
while we

2
lie with our limbs
          moist and dumbed
in the tall grass of the room,
beneath rain flakes &
thunder horns. Here
there is no time,

3
never a dawn.

4
The room is a castle
of parrots, a paradise
          of song. The heat
of the moon leaps
from the grass rug
into the mouths of two
late night connoisseurs. Butterflies

possess the bathroom and trip
from the shower in bursts of papaya
orange,

their scales absorb the light
and the soapy-taste of flesh.
          The rain is a violin.

5
You part the drapes
to watch the rain from the place where
we don't know who we are.

6
We ask nothing
of the night but itself. Here's to rain
in a drought, which is our metaphor.

7
The first sloppy storm
          in years and we have said
too much, nothing
can change the colors of this hour.

8
A moon cut on the bias,
a sky sewn together by a drunk,

9
shaky moments making up a shakyshaky whole,
think

10
no further. The world
                    starts here.

WEDDING IN THE PARK

Chicken thumbs sliding around in teriyaki,
            apples crouched in a plastic covered bowl,
someone laughing at something funny,
            touching forearms — love could

be like that; oh and blues
            and sunsets, San Diego sweet blues,
a Southern California flab of sunset,
            Chardonnay in paper cups.

You check your e-mail
            like a deer pants for water,
someone swims laps now, (the sweet flip
            for air,) the careless down-stroke,

while seals lying on rocks, eyes blunkered
            like maraschinos, children
digging up castles from a sand prairie,
            it's a Legoland of romance.

See the gardener as
            he mows with blades too dull, his son
pulling squirrel grass; they bend to the task without
            a word, but dab at sweat and smile
between their fingers at each other. You stand in

            a recital of trees today, knees gone goofy,
tongue gone clicky. Your best man runs
            four lanes of traffic to an ATM machine
and a bridesmaid brushes a hard mascara ball

            from the corner of her left eye, you'd like
such erotic blasts of June to lift you higher
            when you wear flowers in your hair
and register for night school. The world

hums its refrain, goes on with its business
— you want it all, you know you want it all.

SHUT-EYE SLEEP

Every shut-eye ain't asleep
Every good-bye ain't gone
—folk saying via Michael Harper

The peregrine falcon can recognize
the voice of its trainer a mile away.
We're looking into the cottony eyes
of a shut-eye afternoon & waiting
for that poem when the top of our heads shoves off
without the rest of us. I'm worried
about finding my daughter's blanket
before her naptime.

I'm digging for words like coins shining
in the dew map of her birth. I tell myself
each day is rife with choices, they're stitched
into the gauze of the storm,
they're boiled in the soup we eat at noon,

but try
stretching your predator neck
while the sky, clean as the sole of a new shoe,
falls down on you &
you're supposed to be Tirèsias.
Prufrock's love song served with the same
          fast lunch tunes you heard back home,
                    Take Out Your False Teeth Mama,
                    Let Daddy Suck Your Gums,

try to write something today. Fire the switch,
jerk the wings, we used to know what
          we're in the universe for. Used to
count every goodbye like small jewels,
          like we were learning something with each
sad final glance, each toss of the glove.
          I've got to find my child's blanket,
got to smooth the bed, close
the window, start a fire, keep us warm.
Goodbye is not gone and the women
will always come and go. My daughter

hears my voice a mile away. Of ten billion
sounds, she knows my voice, a vain
and clumsy trainer holding tight
this girl whose head knows its home
against mine, whose shut-eye sleeps in me.

ON THE ROAD

I'll try to step into my life this morning, gather
the new day in my flight bag, grab the closed fist
of this city, pull its fingers apart, allow its echoes,

its rocking and rolling stories of tankards and trucks,
jade and jazz, knights and saints, to enter
me. I'll try not to ache for the sky bed of home, not

today. I'll try to be here in the now,
in the *now*. I'll climb the wall by the parking lot,
scale the steel of the razed buildings by the river,

count the broken legs of the cockroaches I've crushed
this week, study the diseases of pigeons, write letters
home to Mom, dance barefoot in the first swell of grass

I find, sneak into the Chinese laundry, water the silk
geranium, but here I go again, dabbing at the lamp of October
with my subway tokens and my books of notes in hand,

ruffled in my small romance with indices, which I love
like people. I'm on higher ground these days, can't I see
that? Downstairs in the empty lot bottles and cans

lie in weeds like holy relics and my leg itches, the leg
that bends at the shrine of the Eucalyptus in California, that
likes to lie down on the platinum flesh of the beach and

eavesdrop on the jabbering of sand flies. Maybe a person
can be on the road just so long before all skies
become a hotel bed, before airplanes and airports,

elevators, taxis and strangers become blurred photographs
of themselves, but I'm in New York where the world
meets the world— war and peace, fame and obscurity,

faith and practice, death and dying
take turns with their promises and bright lies.

LARGE DEMANDS AND SMALL BETRAYALS

The great-aunt sits on her bed in her room
at the home in St. Paul. She wears her pearls
and the crocheted hat from her great-niece for the 92nd
birthday, two years ago. Her legs and feet are wound
around with ace bandages, fitted with men's woolen stockings and
propped on two cushions taken from the chair in the hall.
The great-aunt is tracing squares on the blanket with her fingernail
and talking to the television set in the corner.

The niece appears in the doorway. The great-aunt
doesn't take her eyes from the television screen.
The niece enters the room like something spilling
from a tube. She carries a bouquet of flowers the colors
of a bad tattoo. Most times the aunt doesn't recognize

the niece, and when she brings the children
to visit, the aunt becomes electrified, asks
their names over and over until she exhausts
herself. I had to see you, Auntie, sobs the niece.
She places the flower bouquet on the blanket
next to the great-aunt's leg. The room smells
of disinfectant, wool and rotten apples.

Flowers, says the aunt. The niece nods. She has come
today because life here is simple. Lunch at noon, bath at seven,
medicine at nine, and because she
wants to be a beloved great-niece. She is here because
the aunt knew her when she weighed just six pounds, when she was
an above average child, when she won talent contests performing
poems and songs without

knowing their meanings, when she danced for love,
when all the aunties and uncles kissed and pinched
her cheeks, when the world was shafted with copper,
before the large demands and small betrayals. The niece

begins to sway. Her face is disconnected
from the rest of her. She moves her arms
over her head as though erasing a thought
or cleaning a mirror. Auntie! Auntie! cries the niece.
What should I do?

The aunt's face is without expression.
She is like a clear body of water. At last
her gaze abandons the television screen. The niece
sniffs and washes her hands in the air.

The aunt touches the niece's shoulder, her fingers
like small paper boats. Let's watch the program,
she says, and clicks the imaginary control. They sit before
the blank screen in silence except for the sighs and small
bursts of throat clearing from the aunt.

A white November moon appears between
the branches of the oak tree outside as gusts of snow scratch against
the windows. The aunt chews
on a banana. I won't let them get to me, she says.
Her mouth folds around the banana slice. Do you understand? They
can't get to me. She pronounces the words

deliberate and distinct as though speaking English
for the first time. The niece has the sensation of floating
on ice. Gravity shifts in the opposite direction, like
yesterday when she drove the kids to their Daddy's office,
but the door was locked and through an accidental shift
in the blind she saw a woman, her fleshy buttocks,
heard her husband's voice from further away than his spread thighs
and expanse of spine. *I'm in a meeting* he called out.

Endings are not resolutions. The room is quiet now
except for the murmuring of banana pulp
in the great aunt's mouth and a sly wind turning
corners of the house. The niece relaxes into
the embrace of her great-aunt and removes the flowers
pressed against their legs. She laughs out loud
when the aunt screams in a voice to shatter ice:
Are you listening? ARE YOU LISTENING TO ME?

BEAUTIFUL AS YOU ARE

       The father returns to Sicily for the summer
and we see the daughter rushing to the cool place
where he stands waiting beside the carob tree,
her face is spotted pink like velvet
flowers on an old woman's hat.

Then pressed hard against his cheek
their bones, veins, the shapes of their fingers,
their two matching mouths,
skin and blood
thick like the heat of Etna, the girl
is sheltered safe against his bright chest. We watch

      as her hair spreads
like a sunset on their two faces and he says
        you're beautiful as you are. Tears yammer
under his shirt, the voices
of wasted years,— even trees ache for resolution— but
what matter now
      with the happy sprawl of tomorrows
before them. This is how
      I dream it, she says,

      how I've written it down.

                    Leo Jordan —d. 1972

IN SEARCH OF VERBS

Tonight in Los Angeles you feel good,
as if kissed on the lips by something
inhuman, angelic maybe. You imagine
you have been licked all over
by the tongue of God. Visited
perhaps by the patron saint of verbs.

You mark the day with a pen
like when you study the Mobil Road Atlas
and touch with your fingers the place
of your home town in your home state
in your home country
which proves you exist in the universe.

Too many airports, lecture halls,
suitcases; beds smelling like cottage cheese.
Hotel roses stare at you through eyes
of bad art. You want to listen
to the live voices of wild asters, bellflowers,
goldenrods and milkweeds.
You can hear them. They're like family
moaning for attention.

You want to unpack your bags, stop,
examine the real gardens of life,
you want to repeat verbs out loud:
verbs like touch, trust, ask, receive, know

and remember. You head for home,
drive the long needle of the 405 south
to Encinitas, the lights of your car
meeting the lights of oncoming cars
like shoulders brushing shoulders, you
wear your space, your flowers, your verbs

and you're reminded of the marble floor
of the hotel bathroom beneath your feet,
the peacock green
sheen of the carpet, your ill-tempered
sinuses, the sensation
of being born into another morning
on another map,

you recall the man who ate his continental
breakfast danish at the corner table,
how he sniffed, swallowed, gulped
with such vigor — a man
of a thousand verbs. It's yesterday
you search for, you're not
finished with the fiction
of things past, the who of you

beneath the ribs, the one
you've tried so hard to reinvent.

AT HOME

This living room
and the icy edge of the solar
system have a lot
in common. Celestial bodies
roam here, they orbit and create
halos. Your shoes by the sofa
your socks, your trail
of papers. Comets are buckets of nothing
off in space, but near the sun, they
explode — just look at us now
rounded over our books, our cosmic
maelstrom of argument &
allusion. I'd live anywhere with you.

IRON MAN

You are my iron man, my new
and true, the solid of square
of all roots, the man who slit my skin
to release the wound. I am too
young to be loved with so much
healing, to have earned the heart hammer
that keeps its ring, that smoothes
the rips, the rifts, the stumped
plug and mask. You: steel and storm,
bold plenitude, you've done to me
what a desert rain does to the Boojum tree.
When you opened me I learned
to respect the bloom, the burn.

ROLE REVERSAL

The mother sits with her feet in sand
listening to the ocean's hoarse breath
thinking about her daughter who has
left home to live with a man. Two Chow dogs,
cragged with sand and mud like desecrated statues
in the back alleys of Florence, jump her from behind.
The woman falls back, then shouts
at their dripping ears, *Go home, go home!*

The dogs spot a dead seal half-eaten in the sand,
its head and tail gone as if removed in a puzzle.
Some people circle the carcass. They are solemn.
They take photographs, but remain reverent
as parishioners waiting for communion.

When the tide is out there's a yanking of the earth
toward water, a push of waves from the sand parking lot
where salt and sky meet like tourists on a city bus
and an ocean keeps to itself
tucked inside the wheel of the earth.

Ladies wearing broad-rimmed hats
and long sleeves gather shells
and stones, and a man with yellow face hair
pulls kelp from the body of a dead
blow fish. He calls out to the others
for more plastic bags. The mother watches
these things, she remembers when her girl
loved this beach, its rank surprises.

Sea grass floats to the shore fanning the sand
like the hair of a crone. I could braid it,
thinks the mother, braid those weeds
in a turban or crown and wear it to a funeral

where yellow-haired travellers
do the bunny hop and the one-step
with bouncing daughters in white anklets
swinging to the music of the sunset.

A tanned mom & pop with their two boys
toss a ball nearby. The mother writes her name

on a sand castle with a bamboo stick. She desires
the letters to be thin and deep, a banner sinking
straight down to the basement of the world.

O Let my banner dissolve, she thinks,
let it be walked upon by priests
with bells on their toes. She misses her daughter
so bad she can feel China pop out of her skin
and hit her over the head with hand cymbals.

The mother is thinking how the daughter
must still need her, and therefore doesn't
sense the storm rushing in from behind
the sandstone cliffs, doesn't
see the sudden angry growl and ruffle of the surf.
Doesn't notice the sky go black like the shawls
of women in mourning. She's touching her lips
to the back of her hand, she's thinking
of the dead seal, the shells in their plastic bags,
buried sculptures in Florence. She thinks of the ocean
coughing up its dinner on its guests, her girl,

her girl, the- child who thinks she's
all grown up. The summer storm rips open
a cliff. The mother wants to sink in a tide pool
between the rocks with the shining amulets
and slippers and the reflection of her child
safe beside her. The surface of the water
is her daughter's radiant forehead and the Mother
leans to submerge her face against it
when a sternsweet voice shouts from behind
the unsteady sky, Mother, go home, go home.

DEATH OF A POET

"I hear my father's bones stirring...
I hear my father's bones rising ..."
—Jim Allen
"The wind is old and still at play
While I must hurry upon my way,
For I am running to Paradise ..."
—W. B. Yeats

He runs in his bones
& the wind at play today
leans from a hardscrabble sky,
greedy for more.
Look at the hurl of poems
falling off shelves and table tops
like winter coughs,
the groaning monologue
of invincible winds and the sudden
whoosh of words.
      In a splintered second
the poet hurries
on his way and an icy breeze
dazzles the cracks
in the back yards of our lives.
Stirring bones, we wait here alone
at play.

JACKSON POLLOCK AND LEE KRASNER

(Hans Namuth photo)

artists have come and gone since this
morning with Lee and Jack yet here they are
he leaning over his painting
on the floor like a football player
ready to smash his head into someone's
pelvis   maybe break a shoulder
or splinter a jaw   behind him to his left
his wife Lee sits on a stool   her eye
on the stick fat with paint which
he hurls at the floor abyss   she's partially
asleep   her hand leans on a hip
one slipper drips from a toe   the eyes of fate
sculpted by a beady sun crease the wood in the barn wall
the painting on the floor swells as with tumors
Jack is now a dancer   his hip separates
from the stretched leg   he jerks deep into
the paint   we're out of white   out of ivory black
can't make art without black and white
non objective expression of action   ah the
dance   the wondrous flailing
but then they were out of time   out of one another   it happened
so fast when a tree hit back in 1956   when he at once
was no more
and   she sat alone in the cracked light of the empty barn studio
Lee and her work   her turn

LOST IN SPACE

Such a time,
            when stars sleepwalk,
novas, quasars, pulsars,
            black holes
look back and think how strange
            we are, such a time.
To know more about
            the habits of the Crab Nebula in Taurus
6,000 light years away
            than of our own yawns in snowy fog,
            or why we,
blinkered, numb, walked out of love —
            Now how do we survive the cosmos
with faith as thin as crooked webs
            of midget spiders
and car trouble to boot?
            Don't tell us how we tick. Such times of blessed
blindness to the pea-prick nod of Mars and Saturn &
            a millennium that will cost us plenty,
            we're chockful of happiness.

TIME LIMIT

Professional ballet dancers don't fraternize
with students of the art, they have their pride.
It is the order of things. Best, Better, Brilliant,
each in their place like color-coded hats on
a shelf and you practice until your toe shoes are black
with blood, until your childhood is gone and your
feet take on the shapes of puzzle parts. To shun
ice cream and boys for a love affair with
mirrors, to dance solo in a ballet company, chin
lifted high above a chorus of bowed heads,
posture straight as the edges of doors, to discover
the purl of Good and go on dancing, never
to miss what's missing, never to stop what's
stopping; you're on top topping, and you're certain
there is no life but this.

NEVER FORGET

The parents tell their children they love them
more than life, tell them never forget who loves
you best. Never leave us is really what they mean,
so when the parents sit in the back yard gazing up
at the twisted arms of the junipers circling the lawn,
they think about the sprawl of time that separates
them, how the phone calls aren't enough
to plug the leak they say is breaking the skin of their chests.

The parents look again at the branches of the tallest tree
with limbs that have turned to wings, white angel wings
lifting the sky, pushing up from roots of gathered regrets
and the parents see the faces of their babies in this upward
thrust; the mother sees a love like hers that soured jam
and wilted waffles,that came home late and bought the wrong
kind of cookies to Parent/Child night at school. He remembers
growling allowance days and screaming Drivers Ed. Worse,
the thrashings for a simple lie and the betrayal of the split,
when the house tore like paper and nobody laughed
and nobody told the truth.

The wings of the tree spread open and millions of leaves
fight the trail to earth, slapping and swapping the air,
beating against each other, then settling at the parents' feet
where they curl in death. The parents bend to pick one up,
hold it between them, then turn to the glaring eye
of the tree and cry, *But you never had children.*

PLUM PARADE

I'm driving up the hill
on the county road outside town
      when I meet hundreds of giant plums
      marching in neat rows
down the hill. Round, purple marching plums
      slowly moving along, going nowhere really, just down
      the way parades of humans
go nowhere, making lopsided circles through cities
      leaving bales of refuse behind them,
      ending up tired somewhere near the starting point
      ready to celebrate the great journey
going nowhere all over again.

      I am one of the human
parade marchers. Each year I do my high-knee strut
in my gold tassled boots, my body corrugated with sweat,
      muscles like claws— I grin & follow the band,
 twirling my baton,
      and here's a plum parade with nobody
      to cheer them on, their purple heads glistening
like small lakes, moving in the violet sting of sun,
the ripple of their deep,
      purple flesh shining as if polished by kisses...
On they march, in perfect unison, in well rehearsed,
      orderly ranks stretching for miles, as if the horizon
were an open door or hungry mouth.
                    Toothpicks poke from the
tops
of the plums' heads like hats that have been driven
      into their soft skulls, hats
that are not hats at all, but odd little weapons, knives, I think.
                    The marching plums
seem unconcerned. Hey, I shout, aren't you worried
      about a sudden wind or a flush of rain
like human marchers? Aren't you just the tiniest bit
nervous as to how you will be devoured—
      with knives or picks, sliced or gnawed? Hmmmmm?
(Perhaps they'd meet their end by rotting mid-parade,
      their toothpicks pointed high in parting,
              erect, straight up—)

No, they explain without looking at me. It will happen
　　　at the party later, the big party after the parade.
That much they know.
　　　That's all we need to know they said.

PERSPICACIOUS POWER

The story teller knows
the children's names
by touching
                        the tops of their heads,
            knows the innuendoes in their hair,
children with
            voices like translucent bells.
Sea oats and bayberries
fall from a glass ship on the way
to St. Ives. The beach
            removes its party dress so
            the elephant seal can scratch
the back of a rock at the edge of the water
while the story teller creates
            a hundred jillion shining unicorns
pulled by a great white shark
who befriends hermit crabs and snails
            & gobbles toast and jam.
WE are the unknown princesses
and princes of daughters and sons
carrying out the task of wooing butterflies,
            dolphins and elves
            with our beads of commas,
our apostrophes
and wreathes, our songs,
                        our exclamation marks,

our limitless
perspicacious power.

EMPTY NEST

I don't know when I realized
        I had to say goodbye to them
but every time I think of it
        I feel a prick at the edge of my eye
& recall their warm heads,
hair dreamy as summer
        across my face, voices
by my ear like two small
rising suns, Mamma?
Mamma? Hands like
        kumquats fastened
to my shirt, the morning
        sprayed with itsy bitsy kisses,
June&July kisses, can we have
        ice cream? Can we?
Have ice cream, Mamma? Eyes,
        eyes of white sharp stars,
same stars pricking the corners
        of my own now. Who's making
all that noise? I won't be star-
        pricked for long, won't fall down
in summer,
        my life dripping out like bad
fruit—Children?
You two playing tricks
        on your mamma?
Let go, children.
        Mamma can't play. Things
break, edges go
jagged, time creates palimpsests
        which spread themselves open,
        shake loose and
            break away—

THE SINKING OF SAN FRANCISCO

To carry buildings and streets with you afterward
wherever you go ...
Walt Whitman, Song of the Open Road

Gray day in May
forty-eight floors above San Francisco
and three nearby skyscrapers, their noses
poking into the blue
                    are about to fall
to fog. Three steel-blooded ladies,
concrete walls pressed together,
                    windows like rows of teeth, sinking.
Sinking! The tallest woman goes down last, fog swirling,
tickling up the legs, thighs & the fine concrete belly,
                    two flags are shoved in her nostrils
and one in her pouty mouth—down she plunges into the white,
                    sunroof and all.
Quiet as smoke it happens.
                    Bones, teeth, hot flesh, history,
                    vanish. Poof. Three Titanic women slip from us
easy as slicing an orange.
                    See how the sky leaks a dusk of weak espresso,
                    pushes itself up to the window ledge and we can,
                    in the dark,
                    kiss the world goodbye
                    and then rebuild it.

That was May. Now it's December, fat hog of a month,
                    and I'm looking for a responsible sky, one
that suffers the fog to ride the rumps of trees,
but spares the girls. Fog
swallows the city the way Cupid
                    feasts on the unsuspecting,
the cloud-headed, the easy.

LAST ATTEMPT

I ask for
please for coffee please

mosquito wings
line the window edges   a wee

blob of lint is stuck to my lip
fingers gone flat as lettuce   I'm cool

tho   I'm smiling free
my dear   and two teeth drop

in the palm of my hand   amber
rubs between my knees

a breast rolls loose on the floor
like a cheese and this skin

of slippery sap is so hot perhaps
we'll take off our pants &

lie down on the tile   you
make yours Chablis   some toast

what I desired most
was to see your mouth again

to hear your milky voice   touch
the back of your neck   try again

the door wants to come in and
will it ever rain you wonder   we're

stunned and imprudent to think this
was a good idea   the table

says NOW is the loneliest day
of its life   when it's over

it's over

PLEASURES OF LIFE

In the house across the street
a man and wife
take off for Baja on weekends
without their teenage boys
and when the sun erases itself,

our street lights up like an electrical accident
at Legoland. The sudden thump and clap of music
stuns the neighborhood the way toes
curl at the thought of surgery. Gardens front and back

experience a fresh ache which worries
the birds of paradise, window glass shakes
waking the cherimoya, house keepers
don't know whether to padlock the doors
or dance. Three square blocks of dogs

whine like cats. Laughter stirs the ivy, spreads
in layers along the creases of the peeling
eucalyptus trees. Blue smoke dusts the burnt heads
of the bougainvillea against the wall, smoke
that sticks to the dieffenbachia, bed sheets

and hair brushes. It chokes the necks of the fine
homes known by Thomasville furniture,
tasseled pillows and big freezers. Then
the yelling. Opening and closing
of doors, the slapping of fists, always the same
words—f you man, f you bro,
f this, f that, bare feet on pavement,

someone throwing up on my grass,
making out in cars without fenders
and tires as big as minor lakes, something
breaks, something's on fire & next
morning a wet sofa lies on its side
at the curb like an etherized

patient. Bouquets of toilet paper
 bloom in the fichus trees. Holes gouge
the four o'clocks and hydrangea. The boys
are asleep on the lawn exultant with

hangovers. They lie pink and bent
like shrimp in a bowl. The man and woman

return with their straw hats and souvenirs, he
shouts at her. She shouts at him. Voices
flicker & dim, they just want some pleasure in life,
isthat toomuchtoask? The earth's unravelling minutes
catch in the stern stare of the clockeyed new day.

MINNESOTA FEBRUARY

Don't think the cold
complains. Winter has its resolve
as stars stiltwalk across
the night and morning sleeps in
later every week. Don't think
a single yawn or sigh
while blinkered numb, the ducks
are gone, birch and pine
alone hold up the sky. Catch a faith thin
as the crooked web of a midget spider
needing love. Open the sound
of creaking snow, arms
of silent determinacy, trek in the gauze
of its sleeves. The trail ahead waits
for the squeak of boots, the deep line
of footsmiles, the tink of ice hair falling
from branches. I've searched
myself each winter, hunted
for the balm in storms
where afternoons rise up
and flatten like wood smoke
and sotted fur. Waited
inside the ring of night as the pond
froze, the wind striating its skin
like pillow imprints on a sleeping cheek.
Don't think the florescent flickers
of mornings and noons dissuade the bite,
the snap, the longing for the rake of Spring

THE SURPRISE

With so many whys and huh?s
and not knowing which way to turn
she stepped in a hole
in the ground and watched her foot
disappear.

The topside foot, still connected
to her body, had less to do
with its partner missing
so it began scratching at the ground
independent, yet spongy
when suddenly

two of its toes wore off
and a dog carried the bones
away in its teeth. The foot,
now only part of itself, imagined

being a hand or an eye,
a body part that got things
done, to be a train
humming across the landscape,
hauling accumulated deaths
through tunnels and across bridges,

touching three states in one day,
counting wheat fields from the coach,
shouting faster, faster, creating a roar
on the order of chewing on stone. She wearies

of standing, refuses a seat. Imagine
the racketty-clack, the rush & push
of a stunned single-footer — next came
the marvelous hoped-for jerky

jolt of a leap, the sort that yanks
off a ream of skin before landing. The foot
broke loose and glinted upward
which is what happens when
happiness catches you by surprise.

STITCHES

I'll tell you how stinging cold it was
that last winter in Minnesota,
how sparrows got lost in the sheets
and ice hung in strings from the sink
when the kids played
in the truck and it rolled onto Silver Lake Road
where only prayer could save us— God
and snow mud. but there was a dead dog
on the road, too, and me without
a spa membership. The guitar lessons
had run out and one ruthless geranium
clung to the window ledge by the curtains
I sewed myself, and my little girl
holding my legs crying
Mommy I'll take care of you
and him killing the door.

Oh Spring can be cruel
to linoleum. My tears
of plaster ruined the towels
that closed the gaps in the walls
where he stuck his fists
in our rented house by the lake
where we didn't have
the time of our lives.

Children's faces
like small dusty apples
in December
when the snow turned
bloodstain brown and
I promised to be a grown-up
before they were.

STARTING OVER

Summer nights when the sun
always came up too soon   us dancing on rooftops
in the warm tar singing Lady Day songs
to a city a hundred million miles beneath us
filled with make believe I can't find now
but I did go back to school   I did start over
I should congratulate myself   ride a blue pony
to the dance   dig up a nut clam in the sand
at the beach with my nose and thank the life
I lost and found again   I ought to press my cheek
to the road that led me back to today   I ought to
cover something with kisses—

Once there was a woman who wanted to cover the whole world with kisses.
She woke up early in the mornings and began kissing things around her.
She kissed her bed post, her cozy quilt, her coffee cup, spoon, the butter
dish, her boots, things
she had hardly noticed before. She became delirious with kissing.
She rushed outside into the early light of day ,
began kissing everything in sight. First the tree by her door,

then the wall around her house, garden hose, the road with
all its pebbles and ruts, cars parked at the curb, the post man,
the baker, the policeman on the corner, a passing dog,
a stray parrot—

On and on she went, kissing walls of the schoolhouse,
all the books in the library starting with ART
and ending with ZOO, she kissed the eager faces
of children, old men's noses, doctors, actors,
tailors, forest rangers, poets, ship builders. She went
to the desert and kissed the insects and spiders,
snakes and lizards, cats, rats and bats,

birds and foxes. She went to the Grand Canyon and kissed
the sandstone capped temples of Shiva, Isis and Osiris.
She kissed shale ridges and the red walls along the trails
forged by bighorn sheep and deer.

She kissed the mossy alcoves along the dam, the pine trees'
royal arches at the bottom of the canyon,
the jagged grottoes and queen's chambers
carved in rock. She went to the cities and kissed

air conditioners, hair driers, television sets, electric can openers
and electric guitars. She kissed the chestnuts roasting
on propane fueled burners on street corners,
the orange glow of traffic lights, she kissed the brown stained fingers
of office workers huddled in doorways
smoking cigarettes, kissed newsstands and sunsets,
theatre lights and bus mechanics.

She drove to the harbour and kissed the Statue of Liberty,
took a train to Minneapolis and kissed her daddy's grave. Flew to Paris and
kissed the Pompidou. Traveled
to Munich and kissed the paintings of Gabriella Münter.
She kissed the volcanic rock giants of the Easter Islands ,
slid along the glassy glacier floors of Alaska kissing
ribbed sheets of ice. She dove to the bottom

of the ocean off the Florida Keys and hitched a ride
on a loggerhead turtle and kissing him gave him
the name Jo-Jo Peach Jam, she kissed a Texas drummer,
a San Diego art cowboy. She kissed the memory of every teacher

who ever said well done, she kissed the kisses still wet
on her lips of all the lovers who lost sleep
at the thought of her, the boy named Darwin
who taught her she was more than a thought. She kissed

and kissed. She kissed the lakes and pools of Minnesota
where she learned to tap dance and write, kissed a Chicago museum
director, a philosophy professor in Maine, the priest in Guatemala
who knew love costs more than dying.
She kissed the place where you are now. Where you are now
is lathered in kisses. She kissed everything you're touching.
The book in your hands.

> A smile drips from the face of the sky
> like runny old people food—it forms
> a wet ribbon that is dawn
> and looks like oatmeal   The sky
> is full of oatmeal today   I'm spooning
>
> my life from its slippery foam   I'm
> dancing the moon, I'm not ready
> to die   dancing my holiness   dancing
> my woe   dancing my solitude   my extravagant
> economy   dancing to the end of love   Below me

the world frowns itself deeper
into its sleeping bleached dark   Who will
come with me to the dance?

Wasn't it you who lived inside the sweet flesh
of the clouds with me?   Wasn't it you
who slept with me in our cabin
of the wind?   Didn't we sing with the rain
in its beaded halls? Oh here

I go again   gathering my winters
in the old kit bag   catching those wayward
spinning prayers   I'm riding the blue pony
to the dance   I'm watching the hazel eyes
of the morning from the roof   I found
a nut clam in the shape of a marriage &
I've just begun.

POLITICAL MOVES

Ever think you're turning into a tree
and you're the only person
in the world who knows
how trees hurt?

The magic of language to her throat, the tree
of her body. She was now his,
she'd never detach the scrub
and shrub that grew at his feet.
He was naive,

a fool.
He should have gone down easy,
no fuss, no tiresome protests. She went about
letting folk believe he was the real enemy,
not her.

They took their meals
from the plates of barrio children,
made laws that left fathers lying
in the steets and mothers
desperate for work. Critics said

it was a bad love affair
that caused tourists to return
to their homes, avoid the beaches,
re-route their lives, a love affair
that built a fortune, made charging
fees for sunsets seem reasonable —

which goes to prove,
we're sagacious as fleas.
A mother tells the army,
give me back my son. Didn't she
understand? The world doesn't
expect big things
of itself.

WRONG HOUSE

A girl knocks
on the old woman's door and asks
is this where the party is?

Party? the lamp is tired of the light.
the window
wants quiet. The woman is ankle

deep in cat hair and dead insects, her radio
is on the blink, but she has tea in the cupboard,
some peach wine perhaps? So many
stories of glory and shame beauteous
in rust. The girl lifts a hand to her mouth,
THIS MUST BE THE WRONG HOUSE.

                When the old woman's
daddy threw a party you could
hear it clear to Cleveland, a live orchestra,
ladies dressed in cerise and navy,
men in bow ties and shoes shiny as blisters,

oh she was fetching in her day, fell
in love left and right, then once
too often in the gala of the glad: the duke,
the prince, the man in medals and a war
that stilled her rooms.
No, my dear, there's no party here.

The house flexes back into its bones,
the lamp tweaks its sore eyes, its raven
ears. The chair sits down, the table
pulls up. Go away! they shout to the girl.
But the old woman pays no mind. She follows
the girl.

The house brays irate.
                The house yowls furious! We don't allow
entrances and exits here! Get back inside! The house
has a voice like her father. The old woman
hears music in the black den of night, she feels
the souldance of faeries and suns, and oh
how the icy unknown
raises its arms to her, and how
                the old woman dares, she dares.

UNDERNOURISHED

My friend has a new lover; she's
riding bliss like a prayer, her face
could light up a silo. She uses words
like soulmate and miracle although
she has a husband at home and I'm cogitating
on her four not-now kids and the twenty miles
                of toilet paper they stunned onto
                the tree outside Sav-N-Shop. Their
mother is twinkling phosphorescent,
skin like she's been chewed on
by ticks, eyes rolled up, beamy, he (the lover)
is a beautiful human being, she didders.
                But that tree was the only one in the entire
                shopping center. Always
people around to destroy what ought to be,
a few branches, some leaves, shade enough
for half a car and one or two hungry
crow, an undernourished liquid amber is all,
but still, the only thing alive in all that
asphalt. She's teary
                now, overcome with the sheer
                joy of her love life and I feel lonelier
than scalp itch. Tonight
I'll dream of a hundred million brides
in their white sassy wedding dresses
running loose on crests of crimson hills,
skirts in flight like ignited doves,
                glorious pollution, I'm sizzling
in voids, in macrocosm dreamfire.

WEIGHT OF THE ODDS

An ocean
has no privacy. People
poking around in it all the time
like dancers at a wedding
rushing for a twirl with the bride. Mostly
we play alone among the fishes,
gold winged and riotous. Do you
want to join these lovers of the deep-delicious,
the blue-wash brine & scum? Want to
tumble in the raucus thud
of an undersea choir
and surrender to the fantasy with me?
We can
nosedive the tangleweeds of itness
& innerness,
a force
equal only to its weight.

BAD JAZZ

Tosca
had but a couple measures of music
to make her decision before taking the leap
from the parapet of Castel St. Angelo
and I'm staring at the stretched body
of my life pressing against my cheek,
shaped like your hand. The ledge near
for jumping,

I'm drawn to you like frost on stone,
the white drip of winter
moves across your face.
                You're as close as the moon.

When Tosca knifed the villian
Scarpia, she became a heroine,
a woman of courage. Once
I climbed the summit of the Zugspitze,
sat dazed in the parade of sky with a lone
black hawk, voiceless as I, perched
beside me paralyzed in the absence

of earth. Last summer
I swam the Mediterranean
in a storm and had to be ferried from an island
off Positano in a fishing boat
of vongole, nets, and chattering fishermen.
We shared a moment of resurrection
in the crypt of those waves, like the hawk and I.
                A woman of courage.

Now you'll board the train
for Milano with your valise of woolen
sweaters, socks and souvenirs.
I will remember you
                lifting your valise.

Last month
at a gas station in Los Angeles
a woman with no shoes rushed at the cashier,

plunked down a fifty dollar bill
and demanded her winning

Quick-Pic Lotto tickets.
She frowned at me as though I were bad luck,
and said, *somebody's got to win, get it?*

Back at Piazza San Marco,
I imagine that woman flying
overhead, high on another
ten million-to-one long shot.
Tosca, floats above as well, forever
airborne, and then there's you

rooted up in the blue. O, I want to *get it*
so I wait for the sun to rise
with pigeons who moan
like bad jazz. Canal wind gathers
the piazzetta in its teeth, the campanile glares
sore and brash behind me. I reach out my hands

to the bottom of the sky
from the Zugspitze where the Alps
stretch to Switzerland. People are always taking
chances. Tosca's slain Mario lies preserved
in snow. I wait for the first strains of an overture
to begin again.

WHEN IT'S TIME TO GO ASHORE

It's no easy decision
to risk the trip
back to earth.
I lose confidence
midway through
the place where
the sky bends
like the neckline
of a ball gown and I often
drop the needle
of my compass
pointing my flight path
down as the dawn creases
the surface of the night
and I feel it gripping my back,
my beak, it's in the iced red
of my eye
and I'm falling fast. I once
thought stars were blades
of pen knives and the sea
was a long black tongue.
I believed stars could cut
the sea in strips to stuff
in the pocket of heaven
where I'd glide free and easy
one day, open my wings
and caw till kingdom come.
But a seabird needs the
lightning shore for plankton,
and I need the thunder fit
of creature love.

WHEN THEY COME FOR ME

*My love is so deadly it picks
the locks of your words...*
--Richard Jackson

When they come for me
I'll be ready, I'll be lighting green candles in the folds
of the red and white tents on the streets of Venice
where at night the dampness chills the teeth &
a stirring of rats can be heard beneath the low slung
window sashes of souvenir shops.
Gondolas in black water bump together
like old men intent on sleep & I know for certain
when they come to get me the candles
will lose themselves in the walls of agate & torn stone.
Mothers and fathers will cover their faces, they will
beat drums and wait for sons
who steal wallets and purses on the vaporettos.
They wash the heads of carnival dolls, fry their
bread in olive oil and it does not occur to them that

I am ready,

that there is a love so deadly lighted bridges fall
from my breasts. When they consider my legs,
the apple on my tongue, the invisible plums,
the water of this contaminated canal will sprout
with words, tourists will fall faint as they move
like spiders laying down their hard-earned lire for souvenirs
and trinkets of glass.
They kneel
in chapels of pier spume, they eat cold buns.

I'm so ready
that when his fingers slip next to my skin and the
flare of his shirt cuffs graze my throat, when his lip
walks the distance of my face and his
mouth is a mess of rain in my hair, I'll remember

I owe the night no stars.

And when they come for me they'll find
the candle between my teeth, I will have lit
my mouth, my face a flaming steeple,
the fire in my gut an embolism,

for I am the brass hearths of the Gritti Palace, the
Cafe Florian crowded with visitors who smoke, I
am a concert of bronze, and I am the bonfires on
corners of Calle Racchetta, I am a woman ready.

I am burning. Let them come.